today i will take a nap
and drink two whiskies.
i will search for meaning
tomorrow.

(page 39, "the meaning of life")

also by robert martens

city of beasts (ekstasis editions) 2019
hush (ekstasis editions) 2016
little creatures (ekstasis editions) 2013

finding home

by
robert martens

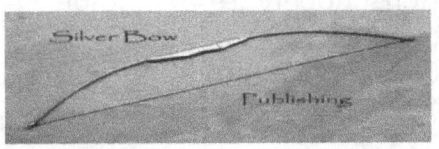

Silver Bow Publishing
720 Sixth Street, Box # 5
New Westminster, BC
CANADA V3L3C5

Title: finding home
Author: Robert Martens
Cover Art: "A Special Place in my Mind" painting by Candice James
Cover Design: Candice James
Layout and Editing: Candice James
ISBN: 9781774032398(print)
ISBN: 9781774032404 (e-book)
Publisher: Silver Bow Publishing 2022

All rights reserved including the right to reproduce or translate this book or any portions thereof, in any form except for the use of short passages for review purposes, no part of this book may be reproduced, in part or in whole, or transmitted in any form or by any means, electronically or mechanically, including photocopying, recording, or any information or storage retrieval system without prior permission in writing from the publisher or a license from the Canadian Copyright Collective Agency (Access Copyright)

ISBN: 9781774032398 (print)
ISBN: 9781774032404 (ebook)
© Silver Bow Publishing

Title: Finding home / by Robert Martens.
Names: Martens, Robert, 1949- author.
Description: Poems.
Identifiers: Canadiana (print) 20220419515 | Canadiana (ebook) 20220419531 | ISBN 9781774032398
   (softcover) | ISBN 9781774032404 (Kindle)
Classification: LCC PS8626.A7687 F56 2022 | DDC C811/.6—dc23

Dedicated to Leonard Neufeldt,
who, with unceasing kindness,
encouraged me to write.

Contents

leaving home

a brief bio ... 11
gulag: johann enns ... 12
holodomor ... 13
slaughter at starbucks ... 14
refugees from/to... 15
found poem / notes / memoir ... 16

home dismembered

dismembrance day ... 19
exile on remembrance street ... 20
little folk ... 24
deep state ...25
tamed ... 26

stories for strangers

worker of the year ... 29
walking in st. petersburg ... 30
etiquette for shoplifters ... 32
hamburgers in paradise ... 33
eleven screens ... 35
rostrevor, northern Ireland (for dympna devlin) ... 36
this poem contains hazardous material ... 38
the meaning of life ... 39

the redemption of routine

a day in the life of the universe ... 43
god's barkeep ... 46
newswoman ... 478
the coffee chronicles ...49
the sliding sea ... 53
prospero's resignation ... 54
smirk stop start again/slip strain ankle sprain ... 55
the drunkard's lullaby ... 56

anxiety alert

anxiety is the dizziness of freedom ... 59

poetic interlude

behind you ... 67
naked apple ... 68
waiting for postpostmodernity ... 69

reclaiming home

yesterday ... 73
new year's night ... 74
irreconcilable ... 75
the vanishing ... 78
in an irish teahouse ... 82
blacktail ... 83
toad ... 84
our daily bread ... 85

journal and signoff

a journal of the covid year, or covert 19 ... 89

leaving home

a brief bio

hunger is necessary for words, for lament,
as the past filters away,
vanishes into fog.
which is swirling over the dykes today,
on a chilly january morning,
snow threatening,
vedder mountain as blue as that
which can't be spoken.

the dykes, strengthened,
after the great flood of 1948,
another traumatic event
in the lives of my russian refugees,
after the holocaust of the bolshevik revolution,
after fleeing with enough to survive the day,
and finding this valley, rainy and warm,
a river ran through it, and they built a village,
a replica of what they'd lost
in russia, their motherland.

my childhood was heavy with their grief.
with their bitterness too,
and the control that tainted their souls,
one way, go this way, they said,
yet we were loved. they were hungry.
embrace found a place there,
and today i'm walking the dyke
that's holding back that flood of grief,
and vedder mountain
with its stone silent gaze,
and all those people gone,
and memories of the west wind
that blew freedom,
and farmers in the damp,
and grandmothers with shawls,
and the minister saying,
go in peace, you are blessed.

gulag: johann enns

how could he tell it, how,
no words for the impossible,
his family loaded into cattle cars, transported,
thrown into the siberian wilderness.

build your shelters, said the
guards, *find your food*,
and they starved, and froze,
and he, of all his family,
finally alone, how to understand
the hammer fist, the sickle fingers,
red, red, until one day,
in that limitless death camp,
one day he meets god,
and every leaf glimmers
and every bough stretches to heaven
and his footprints in alien soil, blessed,
nothing matters, he will rise each day
to the routine of torture,
he will speak gospel
to the thugs of state,
because what can contain him,
the impossible
shattered
this blinding hour
and forever.

holodomor

you have performed well,
brothers and sisters.
you may retire in good conscience.
when torture was demanded,
you practised, and practised again,
that the subsequent object
might feel the greater pain.

you rode the trains,
worked eighteen-hour days,
ensured that the entities
under your direction
died of hunger, slow deaths,
grain by grain,
red, red for glory
and kindness, and blood.

your timing was impeccable.
the knock on the door
five minutes past midnight.
the impediment sentenced
to precisely controlled conditions
in ice camps. admirable work.

you commuted home
to your families,
raised your children with love.
you taught the rest of us
the honour of razor-wire discipline.

you have our gratitude.
we wish you peace.

slaughter at starbucks

everyone's got a screen.
phone or laptop,
their eyes with that peculiar blank,
one young guy with a stack of books,
but a screen has stolen his attention.
paper cups, plastic lids,
a customer line-up that never ends.
one table left. i grab it.
this is one corporate coffee house
that won't need to worry about profits.

now, witness this anomaly.
i'm sitting with a self-righteous air,
reading a crumpled typewritten german text,
eyewitness account of anarchist brutality
in mennonite russia, 1919.
rapes, shootings, limbs hacked off,
babies sliced with sabres.
i look up occasionally to break the mood,
to bathe in the hum of conversation,
the beeps and tones of electronics.
the couple next to me
are so engrossed in their screens
they drop their plate of edibles to the floor.

this is ... is this the norm?
boredom, laughter, caffeine highs?
or, perhaps, the slaughter of innocents,
far away? so far away?

i toss my cup, walk out
into a clear canadian autumn morning.
an election's begun.
speeches, promises, fatuous talk.
i'm not sure, but I may be feeling grateful.

refugees from/to

they travelled, then,
only on special occasions:
a crowning, a drowning,
wineglasses hoisted for three days.

a dog at the door of the inn,
and the host spattered
with the grease and grace
of her kitchen.

in the morning,
they followed the road of thieves,
beasts watching from thickets,
ancient eyes red with suspicion.

they travel, now, refugees
from archaic tyranny,
to the sleek glass city
where boredom never sleeps.

the old hound, fatter now,
on a long leash,
walking city parks
and steel streets.

morning means
the limos of money men,
all beasts long fled to the north,
where the bones of children lay.

they travelled against their will,
slept with the dog at the door,
dreamt of a city ...
that never was.

found poem / notes / memoir

a rainy day valley / a mountain with bears /
a village of sorrowful countenance /
cows and cowshit and tall grass heavy with dew /

a single central road / a church that emptied the village /
hymns slow & deep & four-part harmony /

a church school / a grandfather gentle as a rainy day /
refugee legends / friends talky and earnest and innocent /

a village of wanton control / a village of unthinking generosity / black suits & polished shoes & visiting on sundays /

the city just over the mountain / a hymn that rumbled the earth / a rainy day valley /

lonely attics & lonely nations & rain corroding / a stockade of high-rises / here, now, a heartful of rain /

long hair & striped jeans / certainty / love is the answer / university shutdowns & students deciding / crossing the border & throwing stones at cars & throwing stones at cops & the thrill & the knowing this will never end & and it ended /

the routine of old days / work & love & beer / sleepless nights & visions of utopia of rainy valleys free of heartsick /

regretting the day / consuming the night / starting over starting over starting over /

joy in a single human soul / peace in a universe far away / the routine of new days / a smile a flicker a shot of whisky a few words & sleep /

home dismembered

dismembrance day

remember
you said
on this day of marches
speeches and rain

remember
vimy
passchendaele
when our nation came of age
when our lads –
i'd rather abide
in altered history –
when our lads at
vimy
passchendaele
turned their guns on their officers –
fuck you sirs
we're going home –
and transport ships
took the boys back
to their farms their cities
their parents
their miraculous routine –
because
a nation built
on the murder of children
is a turd
on the polished floor
of parliament

exile on remembrance street

A ram, caught in a thicket by its horns;
Offer the Ram of Pride instead of him.
But the old man would not so, but slew his son,
And half the seed of Europe, one by one.
- Wilfred Owen

i

herod/salome

remembrance day
was a final lurch of lust

a king in silk suit and tie
posed in honour of dead children

the court assembled
over wine, gossip, speeches, schemes

she performed the seven veils
having failed dancing class

the king and princess
leaned backwards naked and pure

their orgasm pulsed the nation
stiffened the march of resolve

how good to die, we said,
at the feet of the beloved

ii

the streets in winter

yesterday was remembrance,
today the winter sun is prophecy,
clear and white.

let me be plain.
poetry may obscure.
our lives are war and peace.
our boys and girls
were murdered
in the trenches,
and parades,
and fireworks,
and prayer.

plain. clear. white. poetry.
on our days off,
we're taking to the streets.

iii

up yours, sir

oh! it was a lovely war
said the henchman said the whore
those were the days of gold and lust
this lovely planet burned to dust
let's do it all, it all again
let's sell our enemies to our friends
bring out the guns, recharge the drones
rain blood and money on their homes
send boys and girls, send old and young
send flies to nestle in the dung –

wait –

remember the hate that haunts your heart –

remember your knee bowed to the king –

the world won't change, just do your part –

have patience, son – that's everything –

no my lord i shall not wait
i'll war on murderous estate
i'll take my hate, submit it whole
i'll wear it proud into my grave
unredeemed my paltry soul
but war shall be my spittle slave

iv

ends with a whimper

the king is sleepless tonight
the princess is bored with his tricks

his orgasm plundered the streets
deathless his city in dream

the court is vacant, dark
the throne is wet with betrayal

the fatigue, the poor soul
the king is sleepless tonight

his trains, his labour camps,
his lovers, he can never
kill them all,

a few survivors hardened by war
will take down his palace, nail by nail,
collapse his bed to rubble,

leave him quivering in the dust,
peace digging at his bones

little folk

rain drifts through his vacant soul...

and mine, framed in glass and steel...

everything was too big for him.
his parents, ogre bulks
that stomped through the hallways.
one with a rock hard chest, and a bellow
that burst from the gut.
the other, standing by.
affirmed the value of big.
meanwhile...

school and city and nation,
he on his knees,
and they... growing immense,
snapping their borders.
everything was too big.
their eyes orbited a red planet,
he couldn't see what they saw.
he nibbled the scraps they threw his way.
imagined citizenship...

no, never. he will mock them,
they are always wrong.
he will blow open the conspiracy
to bind his tongue.
he will build video walls, game the system,
drink the dregs from the bottles they couldn't finish,
oh yes, the bottles tossed to little folk.
everything was too big, and he,
like alice, smaller by the day.
he will anesthetize his mind.

he will message me
through glass and steel...
his voice... an echo...
the hollow beat of rain...

deep state

how do i love thee?
let me count the clichés –

the barbarians are at the gates.
the undead lurch through dead cities.
nuclear terrorism has forced us,
we few, we loyal few,
to defend what is holy.
hairless mutants jabber in the halls of power.
derelict spaceships leak an alien virus.

will you survive the day?
can you bear
the burden of knowledge?

>   *dress slowly.*

>   *it's raining, but it's warm.*

>   *dot this i, cross this t.*

>   *tell your friend of your affection.*

the barbarians want to chat.
the undead were never dead.
nuclear missiles launch
only in your heart,
in your mutant soul.
this alien planet
is calling you home.

tamed

they're all jerks, he said,
all they want is power,
but they're tamed,
beasts of habit like lions in a zoo,
and malice oozes
from the corners of their cages,
so grow fangs, he said,
be honest hunters of the new age,
risk everything in the carrion grounds.

we got stoned last night,
she said, we wanted power
but we got stoned, malice burned
from the tips of our joints,
we're born hunters, she said,
but when the smoke clears,
romantics at heart,
sappy tears,
we're just jerks
hoping for a happy ending.

stories for strangers

worker of the year

oh vall vot kan yoo doo? he'd say,
to a problem on the line,
or boorish behaviour,
or mass corruption at the top,
and i'd say
yeah you're right hans,
but a few snickered
when he turned his long goat face,
his pencil-thin moustache,
and especially those heavy-lidded eyes,

snickered because
he looked cartoon foolish
as he bent over the power saw, studious,
so in jest they voted him
worker of the year,
and discovered that no he wasn't stupid,
he spoke five languages,

and yes they liked him,
hans and his heavy lids
that had seen too much,
a mennonite who survived
a death camp state, and a great war,
and the soviets who forced him to fight,
and the germans who forced him to fight –

did he ever hurt anyone,
it seemed unimaginable,
that droopy-eyed refugee
who had seen far too much –

yes, hans, it will happen, regardless,
hope is foolish, be kind,
the world is an unholy dung heap,
oh vall vot kan yoo doo?

walking in st. petersburg

*"You will hear thunder and remember me,
And think: she wanted storms. The rim
Of the sky will be the colour of hard crimson,
And your heart, as it was then, will be on fire."
~ Anna Akhmatova*

my cousins opted for another palace,
but i had a pilgrimage to make,
and i asked directions at the hotel desk.
anna akhmatova's house?
rummaging, puzzled looks, oh yes,
here it is, on this map, about twelve blocks,
can we call a taxi?

a pilgrimage, though, is for one only.
i walked the russian streets.
yes? no? – i may be lost,
and asked directions more than once.
some, luckily, spoke english.
and there, this must be it.
barely noticeable, a passageway
into a courtyard, green and warm,
and found a sign, in english,
open at ten.

a backpacker for years,
oh i was prepared, pulled out a book,
read in that leafy silence,
until a woman walked by, keys in hand.
then another. and how pleased they were
to see me, a canadian tourist
who knows our anna.

i was flattered.
entered a noiseless, shadowed space.
letters, books, dishes, notes,
all neatly arranged.
i spent an hour there,

still feeling the jetlag,
trying to take it all in...

and how that broken heart moves me.
what pain suffused that room.
what fierce resistance.
a woman who stood in line each day,
bread in hand, hoping for contact
with her jailed son.
as the gulag spread like plague.
as her friends memorized her poems,
words too dangerous
for the page,
for frosty air,
for streets beaten down
by henchmen.

she survived stalin.
she betrayed, argued, controlled,
wrote lines that were steel hard.

i could have loved her.

etiquette for shoplifters

her smile is bright, brilliant, blonde.
i'm buying a bottle of rye
for a weekend with the boys.
and she must be exhausted,
standing erect at the till
through the new year rush.
yet the smile is genuine.
that'll be a grand total of – she says –
and the smile has vanished into history.
the abrupt whoosh of the automatic door,
a shadow figure behind me, and out,
out into the parking lot,
muttering *sorry* as he runs,
bottles of booze clanking
underneath his long, long coat.
knee high socks. shorts, though it's winter.
and running, *sorry sorry sorry*,
with a half-crab waddle,
a thief with a conscience
running to nowhere.

so why's he allowed in here? i ask,
well he won't be anymore, she says,
probably homeless, i say,
and she, *yeah yeah, i know* –

what's to be done?

have a good day, she says,
and the smile is back,
brilliant and blonde as ever,
you too, i say –

and he's running, still,
through the musty corners of our minds,
sweaty, dirty, with that
deep ocean half-crab waddle.
gone.... sorry.... gone ...

hamburgers in paradise

no speed limits in the great state of montana,
and within minutes of crossing the border,
we sailed by a gaggle of teenagers slid off the road.
wriggling like embarrassed worms
about to be hooked.

our own teenage driver was undeterred,
screamed past a herd of buffalo wandering tall grass,
oblivious to their near extinction.
meadowlarks burbled yellow,
the high country hummed a slow waltz,
mountains in the east rose with a sober warning:
do not proceed.

militia territory. end of the line for bulky white men
and the muffled cackle of their women,
they knew with the certainty of big sky
that the government is coming,
that one day we'll all wear suits and ties
and business skirts,
and downtown will spread
like a viral gob of mendacity,
that we'll hoard our guns and roses against that day
when the buffalo will no longer roam.
in the village of paradise,

we pulled into a diner, ordered burgers and fries
from a woman dressed in back country sloth,
she shambled back to the griddle
and soon served up three plates
of hamburgers in paradise
with a cheerful *there you go boys*.

native country too. a silence held in reserve,
we sensed the unease of the town,
of our low grade motel
plopped in a vortex of erased history
and eagles and warfare and carved endurance.

montana is a state of mind.
we felt the clash of survival,
of bullets clenched between teeth,
of uniforms and rifles and polished boots,
this was a divided town, but
they seemed to get along, wordlessly.

natives in the bar, sitting alone,
nursing their beer. whiter than white townsfolk,
packing the constitution in back pockets,
drank alone too.

our teenage driver back at the motel,
safe and bored with the cold comfort of tv.

we drank a couple,
where you guys from, he asked,
canada, we said, apologetically,
nice of you to visit, he said,
what d'you think of montana?
and we drank another. we bought him one,
he bought us another.
beer foamed, boot heels scuffed,
country music thrummed from the speakers.
y'know, he said, *the reason
this town is so peaceful is
we don't have any n-----s here.*
he bought us another. next morning,

we drove home,
stuffing potato chips and beef jerky
into our spoiled bellies,
zooming past meadowlarks
and buffalo and paradise,
the rich pure snows of montana
at our backs.

eleven screens

choose a barstool.
order a merlot. or two.
be easy. talk small.

sports bar. eleven screens,
all showing the same game.

waitress in high heels
and tiny black skirt. the game.

after your first glass,
the bar transforms to home.

the walls thump rhythm.
new lovers with each beat.

beyond, money men are drunk
on artificial blood.

beyond, beggars sleep
on streets of salt.

your barstool topples
through eleven screens.
the waitress is calling.

you'd forgotten. kiss the sky.
order another. we're not alone.

rostrevor, northern ireland (for dympna devlin)

dark streets, and the snug looks closed,
but then we hear laughter, and the roar of song
fuelled by guinness.

we knock at the window.
it's long past midnight, but the door swings open,
a young barkeep beckons us in.

beer and whiskey. guitars and pennywhistles.
where you from then, slurs a drunk,
where you from? the local hero is holding court,
his strong sweet irish tenor,
town of rostrevor, the dear best ever.

belfast simmers in my jetlagged mind.
murals, icons, threats, swagger in black.
history is a stone in the belly.

the irish pub is in session.
mandolin, banjo, hand drum,
melodies we all know. or should know.

three women represent the younger generation.
merle haggard, yells one, *bruce springsteen*.
the redhead does a rap softened by her irish lilt.

old tunes again. 4/4, 3/4, broken signatures,
all together now, this is your night, take it back.
history is butter on the tongue.

teach it to the children, says the local hero,
keep it alive, we will be lost without it.

islands, squalls, ancient ruins, farewells.
one more guinness.

a canadian tune, she yells,
and four strong winds take us home,

sad and solitary, history has walked by and is waiting.

we're leaving, needing a bed, goodbye to history.
night will echo the green, the irish march,
the guns and songs of belfast.

a snug and a story, a pint and a tune,
a threat and a gentle heart.

this poem contains hazardous material

my poem has gone toxic.
despite the good coffee,
air conditioning,
nice conversational buzz,
my poem ...

at the next table,
a mother and daughter
ignore each other.
or at least the mother does,
she texts without a pause.
her daughter has a pretty dress
and toy ipad.
she talks.
her mother texts.

in moments such as this,
i rise to the occasion, i appoint myself
judge of humankind.

the mother
packs the phone into her purse,
they push back their chairs,
and scurry out the door
with their to-go cups.

i should write this, i think,
but my poem would be toxic.

five minutes later,
the mother marches past the shop window
with her husband.

the daughter with a pretty dress
      and toy ipad
           trots behind
      .

the meaning of life

the democratic, polite, and subdued men's group
      has convened.

the men's group has no chair.
that would be undemocratic.
and impolite. and unsubdued.

we are discussing a book
      on the meaning of life.

the author contends
      that the pursuit of happiness is superficial,
      that we should choose, instead,
      to pursue meaning.

my mind is in orbit.

yes, of course we should pursue meaning,
      what fools we are,
      this merry dance
      of arrested adolescence,
      chronic entertainment,
      screens, texts,
      couches and beer,
      while the wind blows,
      and the sea quakes,
      and earth's fragile heart
      falters and breaks ...

but, interjects the senior member of the men's group,
      what is the point
      of pursuing meaning
      if we are unhappy?

today i will take a nap
      and drink two whiskies.
      i will search for meaning
            tomorrow.

the redemption of routine

a day in the life of the universe

un/

nothing.
not/nothing.
*
the universe
is a single point.
it will be so again.
*
detonations,
lumps and dark matter
there,
no/where,
a revolving rhythm.
*
infinite galaxies.
time curves beyond gravity.
a decision.
a question.
a planet
of cloud and blue,
of rock and fire.
*
an eye opens
in the deep.
it is searching
for dry land.
*
tooth and claw:
the hunt,
the birth,
the silence,
vaster than space.
the cry of creature
smothered in time.
*
and then a voice
raises its curious head.

thought

is an abstraction.

an aberration.

was there intention
in the un/dark,
the waters of self-recognition
rolling over
the un/deep?

an expression.

an in/spiration.

of course it's impossible,
this burst of light,
the erect spine,
the planet's meditation.

an evolution.

an ovulation.

the cosmos stretches
into the absurd,
into the un/new
un/dark, with/out
edge, with/out
beginning or end,
and the redundancy
of consciousness,
of human.

and in its soul,
the pulsing residue
of the eternal
smile.

24 hours since

he's awakened
by the daily
big bang.

morning flows westward,
the sky's collapse
remains a possibility,
but the forecast is favourable,
and there's work to do.

by noon,
the galaxies have coalesced,
packing time into
red hot space.
he glances up,
puts on his sunglasses.

eternity,
or is it entropy,
condenses into evening,
a word or two,
a warm bed,
and dreams of day well done.

will he remember his loves,
as the sun burns out
one more time,
as the universe reverses
into a single point?

god's barkeep

the homeless gang was
hammering at the
door, yapping in
four letters about
a black hole
in the street, but
he ignored the noise,
poured me another, and
the beer fizzed like
it wanted to be
born, *yes sir,* he
said, *i was marooned
with crusoe, nothing
to do but scan
the horizon for ghost
ships, there was a
depression hung grey
in the air, it was
humid as purgatory
on a slow day, i
tell you sir, we
slept on sand that
sank deeper
by the hour – but
drink up now –
hey we were
rescued, catch and
release, dropped off raw
in the city, anxiety
hacked the smog sir,
blazed graffiti on
our very souls sir,
and the streets
harder than the devil's
lust – i walk
with a brain limp
now, knowing
there's no home*

*and nowhere to go –
well maybe in the
back room, it's
quieter there – another
sir? – here's a
dark one*, and the
beer swirled like
a whirlpool convicted
of sin, *yes sir,
they say that
god lives back there,
well maybe, maybe not,
someone's paying
the rent though,
and that's all
that matters –*
he paused, as if to
think – ponder –
meditate – upon
the speck of dust
he'd missed in
cleanup, and the
homeless gang
stomped through
carrying a black
hole on their
bruised shoulders
and that was
the end

newswoman

missile strikes on genocidal palaces.
rioting on the roofs of office towers.
her tone is appropriately sombre,
each hair is in place.
anxiety ripples the dark surface of my coffee.
the money markets are burning.
asia is drowning. gangsters
chat in suburban gardens.
politicians are watching us
through retinal scanners.
the bankers want our homes,
they will confiscate wives and children.
the internet is hacking itself.
killer presidents pound their insomniac pillows.
and now for traffic and weather.

        pause.   smile.

dead cattle blocking the freeway.
oil showers in the afternoon.

        despite this –
        because of this –

the sun will set tonight
with news of mercy.
i will recover my sense of humour.
she will report global peace.
her hair is mussed, her lipstick smudged.
the earth's scars, she says, have healed.

i'm infatuated,
tomorrow morning i'll send her my love.

the coffee chronicles

i

writing fiction

down the roll of oil-drip streets
red-green flash on half-shut eyes
monoxide stripping skin and steel
and a city betting on futures past

he's been alone, alone at the wheel
headlights behind him lancing the void
the one-way rush down rubber streets
and a city littered with homeless shoes

he's writing fiction at the wheel
the best-sell prose of his haunted mind
a fiction fuelled by his hot black cup
and a city refusing the day's decay

ii

a day in her life

the artist, she told me,
is born to dip into –
to raise – the darkness –
but daily, she said,
and her sip was an afterthought,
daily i'm suicidal.

she lifted herself
from bed, showered,
ate in a 5-minute squeeze,
stepped on the gas,
blistered past traffic
down the freeway,
to her work-desk,
where she clicked on the screen,
fooled the numbers in the data game,
and after gone moments,
broke for coffee –

where over crossed legs
and blue jokes,
she sips from a black mug,
dips into the darkness,
chatters and laughs.

iii

the geology of caffeine

lack of air
has made the city hazardous.

experts labour over the problem
through the night.

the crusts of street and avenue
are an impediment.

digital excavators
slough off sand and soil.

work proceeds in silence.
a regulated dig.

a rush of air
as they hit paydirt.

underground streams,
black and elusive as dark matter.

the mayor reports the findings
on social media.

conspiracies abound
on the darknet, darkly.

nevertheless, black underground streams,
each morning, sustain our shaken hearts,

and the conversation begins.

iv

closing shop

they met at a coffee shop,
he'd finished his fiction,
she'd clocked out at work
and the young server said,

with a sad, dark smile,
we're closing in a few,
sorry to cut short your conversation,
or is it a love affair?

we'll be leaving soon, they said,
as an ambulance howled,
and a homeless guy scrounged cigarettes,
and the streets steamed white as gin.

they sat in that moment, cups raised,
and the spinning earth dripped black,
and the server with mop and bucket
in a shop closing forever.

the sliding sea

they walk, hand in hand,
backs turned to us,
and all the green that ever was
spreads its fragrance
at our feet.

they walk, walk away,
and will we see them again?

they, we, were born
in deep waters.
they walk, heads bowed,
towards the ocean,
and soon
it will roll over them.

over us.

earth is tipping,
it will slide
into the swell,
noiselessly.

and however we call,
they will walk,
backs turned to us,
into the wind white with salt,
into the blinding crash of tides,
and they won't hear us,
and we will follow.

prospero's resignation

he breaks his wand,
he rips his coat of starry blue.
he burns the book of magic.
he takes weariness into his veins.

all around him, the spirits coil,
hiss, and vanish.
he watches the ocean
billow into the deep.
he takes his killer by the hand.

    a moment ago,
    power was the norm.
    it will be done.
    sin and soul
    at his disposal,
    the tempest distant,
    he on dry land,
    the breezes blew
    as he wished.

he embraces his enemies.
he sets free his slaves.
he's caught between two sleeps,
is this a dream?

island birds lift their heads,
how strange, his frailty,
they'll sing the storm
that whistles his bones.

smirk stop start again /
slip strain ankle sprain

slip, stop, start again,
cup of coffee, who's the blame,
slip, talk, repeat the pain,
peer around the wonder wall,
snap into the dungeon cell,
other, bother,
what's the cause,
rueful pause,
start again,
until –

*the smirk the concealed smirk grabs you by the spine
and shudders you down the guilty hole where –*

ease, my child,
start again,
cup of envy, gourmet pain,
every day exact the same,
you're the beast, you're the love,
push to shove,
you're the least and greatest hope,
gracious speaking thunder pope,
this is it, imagine that,
soul's too fat,
every day begins again,
this is it, repeat refrain

the drunkard's lullaby

(first verse)
he ambles in, flips on the screen,
he's entered the mystical by and by,
a bottle speaks his name and he leans back grateful and
　free –
this, my friend, is the drunkard's lullaby.

(second verse, same as the first)
i'll stay, says the bottle, to the bitter end,
to the splintered time of do or die,
he shuts his eyes halfway and the world's nearly gone with all
　its wicked men –
in his soul, my friend, the drunkard's lullaby.

　　　(tricky interlude)
　　　oh it's such a wicked place
　　　and he'll scrub it till it's pure
　　　he'll swallow till he's sure
　　　it has a sexy face

(last verse if not averse)
he's invited all his bottled friends,
he's heard their distant lonely cry,
the bottles speak low no one can touch you here we've
　declared official peace for us and all our kin –
　god's knocking at the door, will someone let him in –
this, my love, is the drunkard's lullaby.

anxiety alert

anxiety is the dizziness of freedom
(Søren Kierkegaard)

i

same is more is better

the same. a reasonable sleep,
awakening. coffee.
the morning news.
and the sun is a razor slice.
the vacuum atmosphere
of an alien planet
sucks out the hour.
a random invasion.
no grounds for hostilities.
my fork is stained red.
a soul is lost
in a city of airports.

stand erect, shoulders back.

no to the bully at the door.

no to the fingernails
scraping the brain.

and this is my intention –
no, my personally guaranteed miracle –
the setting sun
will be a mere ball of nuclear gases
eight minutes away,
the same, my dear,
yesterday, today, forever.

ii

dr. cliché

time heals all wounds, or so he told me,
in that dark night of the soul,
as time trickled out the office window,
time heals, time at your heels,
& he nodded, & took notes,
leaned back with an empathetic sigh,
time heals all wounds,
& you have wounds, he sd,
they will clarify, he sd,
what doesn't kill you
will make you stronger.

i will prove you wrong, i sd,
in that dark night of the soul,
where ghosts wander
through past lives,
weak & meek
& free as lambs
to the slaughter.

iii

man in the moon

a cold blue earth is rising
the american flag is down
the craters old and unchanging
but of course i may be wrong
in the twilight zone of the moon

my head's in the sun uprising
my feet in the dark of gone
the man in the moon's out walking
he'd sell his soul for a song
in the twilight come too soon

nothing to see it's surprising
for tourists there's nothing at all
no breeze no skin no breathing
pick up the phone there's a call
from the rocket fallen to ruin
in the twilight zone of the moon

iv

un/sleep

sleep is a sinking towards her
but tonight the minutes flatline

dreams are a gentling to under
they've clustered beneath your pillow

do you ever wish to be gone?
when sleep is wide as acid?

at the foot of the bed a presence
the tattered angel of glory

she's come a long way to see you
the music of your breathing

sleep is a sinking towards her
her darkened pools of love

v

down / up

when you're down, clean up your bedroom.

when you're down, don't look up,
it's too smug there.

when you're down, drink a cup of black.

when you're down, walk along the river,
say hello and smile. don't smile.

when you're down, reserve a church pew.

when you're down, follow it down,
be kind to residents of the inferno.

when you're down, tell a bad joke to your dog.
leash your dog, walk along the river,
tell the bad joke to humans with their dogs,
smile. don't smile.

when you're down, chew carefully.

that bridge you're crossing is a white thread
over the nonsense of eternity,
and someone's waiting on the other side,
if your bedroom is clean.

when you're down, insert needles
into the kewpie doll of your ego.

when you're down, wash your breakfast cup.

when you're down, step into the rain.
be wet. feel her on your skin.

when you're up, treasure the down,
leash it, walk along the river.

poetic interlude

behind you

the poem fell behind you.
while you lingered.
while talk and tune
diverted you.

the poem was conceived
in spinning galaxies,
spiked and milky,
at the edge of spacetime.
the poem was a single quark.
it achieved liftoff. it sparked itself
through the divine and godless void.
it discovered our solar system,
entered earth's atmosphere,
took a cloudy breath,
fell with the rain,
with mud and moss and fog,
and settled behind you.
it's home.

say hello.
stroke it like a cat.
the poem was born
in nuclear fire,
it's anxious,
treat it gently,
release it
behind you.

naked apple

this poem is ripe, pluck it.
offer it to eve,
to her dewy nakedness,
watch her chew it,
spit out the seeds and blush,
as eden's fences rise
to spear the sky.

this poem is edible, digestible.
it pushes
through the burgeoning world
of bacteria,
through the long sinuous intestines
of the first woman.

this poem has been eliminated,
crapped out, abandoned
in the garden that someone dreamed.
you'll never see it again.
god steps on it, curses,
wipes it off his shoe.

this poem is fertilizer.
if, at world's end,
an apple sapling
sways in the morning breeze,

pluck it. chew it.
spit out the seeds.
offer it to the one you love.
kick down the fences
of eden.

waiting for postpostmodernity

i'm waiting for the phone
to shake my day
i'm reading dylan's lyrics
to measure my soul
the waiting disrupts my rhythm
it's raining again
crows splash through puddles
clouds kiss the earth
my reading spirals
up four dry dizzy walls because

i'm waiting for the phone

i'm breathing a blank moment

but dylan's lyrics are bloody
and pacifist and patient
and they'll be here
when i finish writing
this disjointed distracted deconstructed
                              poem
and i'm waiting
for the rain to stop
but it won't
for global justice to arrive
but that won't happen
for dylan's lyrics
to crystallize my mindless mind –

well –

this is pointless –

and the phone doesn't ring

reclaiming home

yesterday

today,
i'm caught
in the scream of traffic.
this is a city too large for words.
i look between the shockwaves
of sell and buy,
of rich and poor.
an ageless silence
might dwell there.

yesterday,
i watched the fog
of melting ice.
it caught my breath.
a darkness underneath,
ancient as lost souls,
drawing down my words
into bitter resurrection.

new year's night

you may hear the spray of laughter
at midnight.

you may feel the rush
buzzing the air.

you may scent the darkness
drifting to fume.

you may taste the rhythm
pounding your tongue.

but you'll see nothing.
go back to sleep, love.

rest easy. child. newborn.
they're watching.

they will crown your waking
with the honey of joy,

the shredding grief,
the long-lost friend.

you may hear their rhyme,
the mercy of time,

the rising sun,
because all, all's been done.

irreconcilable

        i

and live each moment
as though it's already gone,
      and you
looking back from limestone cliffs
across a dark and angry ocean,
seeing along a ragged shoreline
those you once knew, and loved,
and fall helpless then, into
      those distant souls:

and when that moment,
      condensed
      in a single drop
      of salt sea:

      drop anchor
in the harbour of hungry hearts,
step up, take their bruised fingers,
and live in this unbearable contradiction,
      that everything,
        lost, found,
    the farthest dying sun,
the deepest ocean cavern, glitters
    in the palm of your hand:

ii

and holding that moment,
with love, with care,
of all that's born,
know its fragility,
cradle it like a mother,
for it would fall and shatter
on the hard grey streets
of the cynical city:

while earth moving slow
as a forgotten dream,
while we in our scurry and rush,
our inept uptake
of greedy breath:

risk that moment,
roll it into the practised hands
of gamblers,who wake each day
in cities of unbearable contradiction,
winning and losing,
dying, resurrecting,
in earth's ponderous turn:

iii

and is this unbearable,

that only in contradiction,
only in contradiction,
can your soul fall and rise,
and live another day?

that on the first day,
the gods nudge our elbows,
shyly, asking friendship?

that on the last,
broken by labour,
they gather up our sins
that litter the streets?

that the first
is the last,

and the festering of our malice,
our wrong
after wrong
after wrong,
precisely there,

where all things meet,
where the winds of pure delight?

can you bear it?

will you speak
a benediction?

the vanishing

not fade away

this day is in freefall

plunging through pixel celebrity babble
and blog-incinerated news
and the long sweatless curves
of constipated freeways

   i have a question, ma'am,
   may i ask a question?

through splintered forests
and starving seas
and winds
biting the yellow edges
of dawn

   you have a question, she says,
   ask it now.

a fool's phrases in the poetic breeze,
couplets in the camps of the homeless –

   the earth is vanishing, ma'am,
   may we go outside to play?

galaxies balanced on our fingertips,
our lost, our fading loves

   you may, she said.

trailing clouds of glory

> *beyond the village*
> *and the blue glacial river*
> *the boy found a queendom*
> *for now and never*

the court of poplar groves,
willows bowing at her feet,
the flow of dandelions
down the riverbank,
she said never a word,
in her realm invisible,
her sanctity of berry
and moss and muskrat.

behind the boy,
in the village,
the routine of
work, gossip, growing,
and he shut his eyes –

this is sickness,
said his refugee grandfather,
don't grieve, he said,
the vanishing.

time is on my side

no words to describe, he said,
the weight of growing old.

he'd thought youth was forever,
the red blink of holy wine.

the city's spluttering dementia,
freeways on earth's broken back.

fewer words the better, she said,
they fall like plastic rain.

he busked in a parking lot,
rush hour swerved to avoid him.

the lilies of the field, she said,
vanish like all good lovers.

crosses of dew at his feet,
the faith of morning honey.

the city on the edge of forever

we were born to this –
wires dangling in ignition wind,
rusted graffiti in techno graveyards,
cellphones tossed to deserted stairwells –
will you speak for us?

you were here before the wind,
mysterious in the migrations of time,
vanished now into that good night –

we pushed you to the rim
of urban empire,
to refugee nations
of plant and soul and beast –

> *how much do we need,*
> *just this transient place,*
> *this soil, this seed,*
> *this clichéd conversation,*
> *and argument, and kindness,*
> *broken-skinned –*

and we built this –
cities sanitized by artificial justice,
air-conditioned breeze
blowing in from the ocean,
screens, mirrors,
selfies of perfect bodies –

will you intercede for us?

our mother who lives in heaven,
may we call your name?

in an irish teahouse

unaware of footsteps behind,
the old toddle on.

they balance on bird legs.
the years trail
from sharp shoulder bones.
they're content with bad hearing,
the past is a whisper.

a grey, grey world it is,
and the clutch of red roses
in arthritic fingers.

their canes tap
the rhythm of the hours.

the old wander by a cemetery,
stop at a cross,
yes we knew each other well,
we were astonished
by childhood.

and they stop for tea,
sip with trembling deference,
smile and nod across the table,
they don't hear each other –

but nothing matters, dear,

where stone meets the sea,
and the fog of lives past,
and the whip of the wind,

through the anxious tick talk
we'll toddle on home –

there's always – always –
tomorrow

blacktail

five years ago (mythically speaking), driven from their valley of eden by megahomes on the slopes. blacktail deer, sauntering past my window, chewing on morning glory, tracing a path through ivy. glancing up now and then, startled, but without fear. no predators, except the bulldozers in the woods. and behind them a lurching doe, and it's my turn to be startled, her rear left leg gone below the knee-bone.

end her suffering? put her down? and why would the pain of a single deer divert me from the genocide of millions? nevertheless. i phone the dept of wildlife. i get referred. finally, though, a real voice, *it happens all the time*, he says, *maybe the foot gets caught in a trap, or sometimes*, he says, *the leg just falls off*, and what does that mean? *and if the leg's gone above the kneebone the deer will die, but otherwise* ... so, nothing to be done. a three-legged blacktail wandering the suburbs. an image of distress imprinted on the day.

yesterday (mythically speaking), out of eden, two does, two fawns, glistening in the rain, chewing on morning glory, down the muddy deer trail past my window. they amble on, looking for greener. or, rather, the first three do. trailing behind is that doe, lurching, her rear left leg gone below the knee-bone, and painful to see, but she's survived. thrived. eden is falling with the rain. the perfect clarity of place. the losses, the loves that have no predators.

toad

when i'm exhausted, you said,
freedom is near.

she's the homeliest of water nymphs.
her tongue's a sticky dart.
her eyes, protrusions
from an underworld.
her skin, warty and bulging,
down to her ponderous feet.

when she speaks,
poetry is a croak.

she's the weakest of water nymphs.
her ponds shrink
as you approach. then ...
... you feel your exhaustion.

she has the power of dream.
mud, algae, waterlily,
as you glide into the drift,
as your footprint vanishes
in the swirl
of mist and grace.

our daily bread

morning routine, as they gather
around the breakfast table,
another day, he says,
another cliché.

he drives the pilgrim's freeway,
stops at each off-ramp,
delivers crystal comfort
to the homeless and weary
in their underpass shelters.

afternoon falls like fire,
he signs off at the office,
walks the slums,
carries jugs of water
to the dying.

when he reaches the last exit,
he's home again, and they gather
around the dinner table,
with your permission, he says,
i will ask forgiveness.

journal and signoff

a journal of the covid year, or covert-19

1.

the mall's abandoned.
        you could drive a truck through it, he says.

so we'll fight later, he says,
        we'll fight like it's normal,
        but for now we're one voice.

empty streets. no one's buying.
        as though a deity has lost patience
        and opened the seventh seal,
                and dropped it like a stone.

the sky is falling, and to our surprise,
        it's heavy.

back home again. my quarantined universe.

at exactly that moment, in precisely that space,
        a monster housefly, first of the season,
        buzzes past my ear.

thanks for the reminder.
        it's the first day of spring.

my cat has other ideas.
        she swats, crushes, and eats,
        with a look of inexpressible satisfaction
                on her whiskered face.

2.

    fresh pot of coffee, extra strong.
           the clerk is contemplating
           a five-minute career in prophecy.

    maybe, she says,
           we'll come out of this better people.
           the economy's down,
           but the environment is cleaner,
                when we don't make money,
                mother nature rests easy.

    i'm leaning against the counter,
           coffee cup in hand,
           i'm socially distanced.

    her eyes shine with the innocence of a novice oracle.

    we'll come roaring back, i say,
           and a few of us will get very rich,
                overnight.

    in the morning, our dreams are forgotten.

    yes i know, she says, i know,
           but we can hope.

    laughter at the far side of the room.

    according to media reports, coffee and lame jokes
           make us better people.

3.

the lake is blue as the sky. beatific.
        a west coast cliché.

nothing else to do, so i walk
        around the blue.

                and eavesdrop.

        i was at the supermarket, he's saying,
        i thought i might stomp on it
        and make it a really bad day for them,
        but i thought fuck it.

she laughs. a friendly-laugh that says,
        no i'm not really laughing,
        here, listen to me.

the mallards are quacking
        like there's no tomorrow.

listen, she says, there are good things too,
        we just don't hear about it.

i imagine so. the more we imagine…

later, i stalk the empty shelves
        of the supermarket. hoarders.
        bad behaviour.

a dearth of toilet paper
        and imagination.

4.

there was a group of women, he tells me,
    sharing tea on the green.

there was a man at the opposite window,
    staring.

and there was i, staring at him.

then, he tells me, the man performed feats of imagination
    with his nether regions.

end of story.

turn away.

this is sex in a time of physical distancing.

and yet my love comes stalking,
    stalking.

5.

the rain has returned.
        after an unusual hot and dry spring
        it's here again.

history has returned. the spanish flu
        a mere century ago. our parents warned us,
            we live between storms,
            we are doomed to repeat.

a fluid situation is the official assessment.
        each day is new. each day is unexpected.

but we've seen this all before.

in the marrow of our secret body,
        it's retained, even treasured,
        our grandparents warned us,
        their stories sleep in our bones.

this will be a long day of alone.

are you bored, my friend?

does anxiety afflict you, my love?

everything,

everything returns.

i'll see you on the other side.

6.

one month ago, i might have wept a poet's tears
      over the road to nowhere. but

when no one's on the road, and the economy's shut down,
      are we somewhere? anywhere?

i'm walking suburban streets, rounding a corner,
      when a bearded man on a cycle
      talks while his wheels turn.

how do you like the new sickness, he says,
      i don't, say i, me neither, he says,
      but there was one much worse, aids,
      one hundred percent death rate,

and i heard, he goes on without a pause,
      that this town has the third highest
      adultery rate in canada.

a non sequitur? or is he alluding to
      the lack of social distancing?

don't believe everything you hear, i say,
      and he, yeah sure, you have a good one,
      as he pedals off,

            an eccentric
            riding the empty road
                to nowhere.

7.

no appointments to keep, and minutes creep,
        and my brain has turned to sludge.

because the larger paradigm is

shuttered shops, vacant streets, people avoidance,
        a great anxiety-drenched
              collective yawn.

we are living in our pyjamas.

and the nano paradigm is

my thoughts seeping through mud,
        the swamp at world's end,
        moss, reeds, brackish water,
        a deer sipping at the bank,
        the drone of flies and mosquitoes,
        a dragonfly cutting through the drowsy mist,
        and now the sun remembering a new day,
        and bathers on the shoreline,
        half god, half human,
        and the world pauses...pauses...
        my thoughts seeping through mud...

did i already say that?

8.

and in all this, silence sneaking up behind,
        tapping us on the shoulder,
        cold, so cold:

and in all this, visions of apocalypse,
        batwings, goats-feet:

for those who are natural pessimists,
        all this
                may be welcome.

this flicker of ebony light reveals
        the world as it always was,
        is, and shall be.

my only defence against optimism,
        said arthur miller,
        is my pessimism.

we warned you, they say.

no, we didn't warn you, they say,
        we gave up trying.

my daughter, he tells me on the phone,
        isn't surprised at all by the pandemic,
        she says, c'mon,
        let's just get this over with.

in a corner of the universe,
        a deity strikes a match,
        takes a deep drag
                on his cigarette.

9.

our poem

in the bitter sip of coffee,

in the blood coursing through our fingers,

in a sleepy morning stretch.

within these four walls,
        the poem contains all:
        the swirl of the seasons,
        the turning of the globe,
        constellations shining through the ceiling,
        our poem, peace, silence, peace –

no:

our poem stops here.

we will now have time, they say,
        to reflect, to read, to test
          capacity of our souls. yes,

some of us will have the time.

but i haven't forgotten you,
        crowded into stifled spaces,
        pummeled by noise,
        waiting for the paycheque
        and you just want to sleep,
        and the kids are crying,
        and the need, the want, the need –

our poem isn't worth anyone's time
        until it shits, showers, and shaves.

10.

time has crumpled into a flaccid balloon.

so many deaths. no end in sight.
        this is not the time for a light heart.

but if all you good and bad people forgive me,
        i'm releasing a light heart,
          a fully-inflated balloon tossed by four winds.

during this time of social isolation:

i miss your naïve redneck innocence.

i miss your distracted look while i'm talking.

i miss your stress and hot temper and bad grammar.

i miss your stupid libertarian solutions.

i miss your compassion for people who don't want it.

i miss your idle cruelty.

i miss your infantile cynicism.

i miss your pointless hyperbole.

i miss your ragged neuroticism.

when this is over, let's gather up our sins,
        and celebrate them
          over a bottle of cheap wine.

11.

the usual gallery of suspects at the lake walk,
        and most are practising social distancing
        [cue the police: *don't stand so close to me*].

the guy crazily waving his arms, yelling into his phone.
the silver-haired lady leaning on her husband.
the kid roaring through, with no warning, on skates.

the couple with two teen daughters
who smile and skip and block the path.

[overheard snippets of conversation ...
        9 ... 9 ... 9 ... cue john lennon]

the homeless bearded man who knows misery
        as his constant companion.

the dogwalker smugly convinced of the cuteness
        of her slobbering pet, and she's right,
        nothing like a canine to elicit smiles.

and then the woman cyclist with a red top that reads
        apocalypse fitness centre.

seriously? in the previous world,
we were kids in a candy shop.

a kindly old man paid our bill.
apocalypse fitness centre?

his mother, he told me, always said,
        you've got it too good, it can't last.

the day is cold and clear. the lake's a steely grey.
        geese haven't been social distancing,
        i count twenty-two
        adorable fuzzy yellow goslings.

                walk on.

12.

    she opens her eyes. five seconds later,
          the shock sets in. she'd forgotten.

    no handsome prince, that is a myth.
          within this myth.

    sleeping beauty. her dreams were
          of daffodils and buzzing bees.
          of a sleepy, kind, ancient realm.
          of a cobbled town
          and a river flowing through it.

    five seconds. enough to remember.
          her realm in shock. invisible
          invaders. conquest by stealth.
          such stuff as dreams are made on.

    she climbs the spiral stairs of the tower,
          steps onto the balcony,
          she will address the nation.

    my beloved. wherever you have fled,
          whatever your place of refuge,
          i am there, i am with you.
          in the volcanic swirl of time.
          in the slow burn of the sun,
          in the nether depths
          where ocean meets the constellations,
          i am there.

    i will drink to you, she says.

    and her cup, her golden cup, is empty.

          she can't remember –

                don't worry, dear, he says,
                    i'll pour you another.

13.

and the trumpet shall sound.
        daily, at 7 pm.

a new ritual for life in the brave new world,
        the trumpet is the signal,
        then pot-banging, whistles, shouts, whoops,
        a celebration, a tribute
        to our frontline workers.

and to ourselves, for surviving with good cheer.

on opening night, my cat panics,
        scampers to the farthest darkest corner
    of the house and cowers.
            a feline apocalypse.

a new routine for life in a silenced world.

my contribution #1:
        a yowl at the door. too short.
contribution #2:
        strum a mandolin. g major chord. too quiet.
contribution #3:
        bang a stainless steel pot.
    it's indestructible, but lacks the creative urge.

        final and lasting contribution: a clay bell
            brought from ukraine,
        a sweet and merry tinkle.

7 pm: whisky in hand.
        trumpet. bangs. whistles. shouts. tinkling bell.

my cat saunters away, she has developed an immunity
        to the daily cacophony.
            i laugh. the gladness of it.

7:04: silence. see you tomorrow, yells the neighbour.

14.

i'd meant not to write today,
> but it's easter sunday,
> and the dead return unexpectedly.

my grandmother, she says, spoke yiddish, fled russia,
> and the trip to north america lasted one year.

how can we, she says ...
> this is, she says, the human condition.

greatness has been thrust upon us,
> rise up, my brothers, we few, we happy few.

we're at war, is the message.
> a banner in red and black.

well, i'd rather not, sir.
> i'm a peaceful man. a bookish man,
> given to routine.

my grandmother spoke german, fled russia, was
> grateful for sparrows, and grandchildren,
> and a river valley, and gossipy neighbours,
> and an aching back, and hymns hummed
> while washing the floor.

the war can wait.

today's a good day for housecleaning.

15.

the bread i baked, says my friend,
        wasn't as good as i hoped,
        wasn't as bad as i feared,
        it was like life.

mediocre, he says.
    stop.

    quarantine.

    if only.

because
        these are not mediocre times,
            every breath we take
            is measured,
            we're watched
            by a big shaggy fool
            who lives in the sky.

let's build, together, a world
        without heroes,
        where we will stretch and yawn,
        and grumble that we're bored,
            and say useless things.

like this poem,
        we will be mediocre,
        and delight shall take us
            unawares.

16.

don't speak of world's end
because that has already been

like a stone from the hand of god
blundered upon this world's ancient bones
from a sky deep as the first day
from our lost childhood
which is forever

       which is gone
       when you open
       your infant eyes

don't speak of world's end
       that in this now
       in this beginning
            unfolds into love
            and loneliness
       and you're gone

17.

the poet, he said,
(i said)
is destined to travel alone.

he (she) is a man
(woman)
of constant sorrow.

but now, for a dark and luminous moment,
    we travel (all of us) under the same cloud,
    upon which the archaic god of thunder reclines,
    tossing bolts of lightning on our timid soil,
    and cursing, loud and clear,
    ye shall all be poets.

well, yes, she tells me,
    my husband is loving this time,
    all he foretold has come to pass.

a new dispensation?

well, no, i'd rather not.

the god on the cloud is slack and slobbery, and,
    in some bright hour, blinded by the light,
    he'll slip and fall,
    and drown in a vat of beer.

the poet, he said,

(i said)

is destined to officiate at his wake,
    he (she) will party till dawn,
    kiss and hug,
        and piss and chug,
        and indulge and divulge
    in endless, mindless cliché.

18.

each day is a single breath in this new world,
       someone's lungs pumping it in, out.
       is it ours?

is it yours?

each day is a word, a note, a sip, a glance,
       so alone, lonely,

are you lonely, dear one?

hold to this. embrace it.
       let your grief flow through lost time,

where a god has slept since the end,
       since the final flickering star,

and is aroused by a breath,

and your joy will be full,

a god shall lift it.

19.

i'm phoning you on the bard's birthday,
> he says, just one day after your own,
> do you know any lines?

tomorrow, and tomorrow, and tomorrow,
> *creeps in this petty pace from day to day,*
> say i, *and all our yesterdays*
> *have lighted fools ...*

macbeth, i say, i recited those lines
> from the floor of the amphitheatre at epidaurus,
and every syllable distinct to my buddy in the top row.

> *... have lighted fools the way to dusty death.*

the rain has stopped. breaks in the clouds.
> the weekly forecast is bright.
> governments, local and national,
> are making plans to re-open the economy.
> perhaps we will live on
> as though nothing happened.
> yesterdays. time segmented and structured.

life is a tale told by an idiot, i continue,
> but sorry for being so morbid,
> that's alright, he says,
> happy bard's birthday.

we hang up. see you

> *tomorrow.*

> *and tomorrow.*

20.

this morning
the universe is framed
by a triple-glazed window.

tantalus watches
the expansion of space,
the gravity tugging at his planet.

he's sick with wonder,
he wants to breathe in the glory,
his skin is pale
with the virus
of indoor light.

      a friend is leaving.
      long bones,
      a bed,
      bottomless eyes.
      another arrives.

tomorrow morning,
the universe blasts his walls
into photons. the window topples
into the love that made us.
he's wondrously well,
      our icarus,
he steps over the edge
into pure light,
      into nothing at all.

21.

there's no point. this period does not belong (.)
        in the infinite recurring big bang
        of loving/hating humanity,
        endings and beginnings merge,
        a looped curve of time and space.

these are the days of miracle and wonder.

officials mark the reopening of the economy,
        the cameras roll,
          everything old is new again.

in this weighty hour of awakening,
        i look back from a future lifetime –
        tell me grandpa about the pandemic,
        yes my dear boy,
        we reopened our stale yesterdays,
        and nothing changed,
        nothing changed...

still...
        at the skateboard park,
        the kids have breached the yellow tape,
            laughter and insolence drift
            with the warm spring breeze
            through my uncut hair...

no point. insert comma here,

www.ingramcontent.com/pod-product-compliance
Lightning Source LLC
Chambersburg PA
CBHW072102110526
44590CB00018B/3279